Pariah: An artist's guide to the music industry

Written by: Matthew Rader

Table of contents

For Nicole. I hope my work

immortalizes my love for you.

Introduction

Hello fellow music artist! My names matt. I'm a rapper with over three years of experience and my music has been heard by 500,000 people worldwide. Over the course of this book, I will teach you everything you need to know about entering the music industry. Whether you're a rapper, singer, DJ or Some other musical artist, I believe its absolutely crucial to understand The industry prior to entering it. With a little help from the homies at pariah records, I will cover everything from distribution, ASAP licenses, and record labels, to merchandising, Cover design and the recording process. But first let me tell you about my journey in the music industry.

My first single *Veins* came out March 16th 2019. And God was it bad. It was poorly mixed, the mastering could have been done better by a drunk hippo, and I had no lyrical skill at all whatsoever. So, what changed? April that year I started talking to my good friend Daniel Yates. He gave me the wakeup call that my song was utter garbage. Throughout our hour-long conversation, I realized something really important: I should have done way more preparation before just randomly releasing a song that I wrote and recorded in one day. I had so much potential but such little knowledge about what I was getting into. I don't want anyone to make the same mistakes I did. Rapper Brent Curry and I even started a record label with the soul purpose of educating artists, because there's nothing worse than wasted potential. Since I co-founded Pariah records, I've worked with dozens of young artists, helping build their career by the ground up. You have a lot of potential. If your reading this book that means that you give a whole lot of fucks about what you do, because you LOVE it. You and I both know, there's nothing quite like being able to express yourself through music. It's gotten us through the worst of times.

Chapter 1: The writing process. Bars, Lines, and rhyme scheme

Ah writing. The first step to your journey, is writing your fist song. Now, there are a crap ton of ways to go about writing, but the most effective way is writing to a beat. Play a beat and stay on rhythm. If you don't have a beat but you have a great line stuck in your head WRITE IT DOWN. Then you can figure out the flow and rhythm later. Another popular way to write, is to freestyle. Just play a beat and rap or sing whatever comes to mind, then write down whatever sticks.

Now let's talk about bars. They're crucial to writing any genre of music. Being able to count bars correctly will show you where to place each rhyme in a song, and how to properly structure it to the beat. The majority of modern-day music (weather its rap, pop, rock etc.) will have a 4/4 time structure. You know when a dope song starts playing, you nod your head? Your nodding to the beat. Every four times you nod your head, that's one bar. Here's how you should count a bar: 1 2 3 4... 2 2 3 4... 3 2 3 4… 4 2 3 4. There ya go. That's one whole bar. In rap, the best lyricists aim to keep their flow up for four to seven bars, but as long as you don't switch your flow up every bar, you should be fine.

Now, you can write litirally any way you want, but the most effective way to structure your songwriting is to put it into lines

So, your song should look less like this:

Now look where we are, they told me aim for the sky

but I shot down the stars life finna give me some

scars but I won't stop till I get to mars

And more like this:

Now look where we are

They told me aim for the sky

But I shot down the stars

Life finna give me some scars

But I won't stop till I get to mars

Writing your music into lines not only cleans up the look of the page, but it also Help tell you where the rhyme scheme changes, where to breathe, and it helps you sort out different flows. Super helpful. Ok so what's a rhyme scheme? A rhyme scheme is exactly where you place different rhyming words. Rhyme schemes can vary from really simple to extremely complex. For example, here's the rhyme scheme for my song *Untitled*.

Back at it

Like a bad habit

Finna smoke this

Like a crack addict

Abstract B rabbit

I highlighted every syllable that rhymes. Whatever genre you're in, you'll want to have an apparent rhyme scheme.

Writers block Is always a huge obstacle to get around. The easiest way to get inspiration Is to stop trying! The more you force your music to form, the less quality its going to have. Whenever I have writers block, I've found the best way to find inspiration is to travel. It doesn't have to be far; it just has to be somewhere new. Books are also a great way to get your imagination flowing.

Chapter 2: Recording, mixing and mastering

The recording process is honesty my favorite part of my job. There's no feeling like pressing the red button on your DAW and seeing your ideas come to life. But how exactly do you go about recording? The best way to record is to find a recording studio. If you live anywhere near a big city, chances are there's a recording studio to rent out. The average rates for a good studio are about 45-70$ an hour. Ya. Pricy. But very worth it! With a studio you'll have an engineer who'll mix your song and do some expert level shit with your vocals. And the engineer also knows how the equipment works. So that's a plus. But if you're like me, and your entering the industry with a total budget of that quarter you found under your sofa, then renting a studio isn't really a choice. You'll want a good computer, a mic and a DAW.

You can make studio quality music for half the price. What's a DAW? DAW stands for Digital Audio Workstation. Its an application for your computer that's an all in one tool for recording, producing, and mixing. There are a LOT of different DAWs with different levels of effectiveness. There are five super important factors to consider when finding the right DAW for you:

1: What's my budget?

2: What will I be doing with it? Vocals? Producing?

3: am I good with technology?

4: What can my computer run?

5: what equipment do I have?

I'm goanna say something super controversial: there's no superior DAW. They all work differently for different people, but here are my recommendations: if you only plan on using your DAW for vocals, you're on a tight budget, or simplicity is what your looking for: Use GarageBand. GarageBand is a free DAW software for apple computers. Its free and super super easy to use, and its my choice DAW for vocals to this day. If you have a sizeable budget,(99-110$) and produce more than anything else, then use FL studio. FL studio is a bit more complex, and takes more time learning the ropes, but it really is (by my opinion) one of the best DAWs for producers.

So as soon as you've recorded your song, I'm assuming your wondering what mixing is. Mixing is basically the process of… well, mixing, the vocal's and beat together. The mixing process with every DAW is different but always be sure to trust your ears.

After you've mixed your song, you'll want to master it. Now, mastering is kind of optional. But I highly recommend it. Mastering brings out that crystal clear CD quality. There are different services online that master your music. There are about 13 that ive used, but here are the best:

BandLab. bandlab is a free service that provides Production software, And Mastering that brings out clarity, Enhances the bass quality, and upgrades your song to 24 bit. So ya that's awesome.

Emastered. Emastered is a super good mastering software that has been used by The likes of Taylor Swift, T.I and Beyoncé. The price ranges from 14-40$, depending on the features you want from it

Landr. Landr is another great service that costs about 9-25$ monthly

Chapter 3: what is music distribution?

So, you've finished your song. You wrote it, you recorded it, you got all the legal stuff down, and now you're ready for the world to hear it. But you have one big question. How in the world are you going to get your song onto Spotify, pandora, and iTunes?? Well that's where distributers come in. there are over 100 companies that will distribute your music to all of the biggest music platforms out there. I've used many of them, and I've found that distribution companies are like DAWs: they range from super cheap to really expensive, and your choice depends on what's best for you. Since My song *The Test (Feat. ZZZSomnus)* my main distributor has been DistroKid. With DistroKid, for 19$ yearly you can get as much music as you want onto over one hundred and fifty music platforms, including YouTube, Spotify, and Apple music.

Here are some alternatives to distrokid:

CDbaby. Cdbaby is expensive. 40$ for a single and 60$ for an album expensive. I can't recommend it for singles, but album distribution is another story. They'll distribute your album, get it affiliated with ASCAP or BMI, and they'll duplicate your CDs and get them to brick and mortar shops.

Amuse. Amuse is a free distributor that lets you release music from your phone. They get it on every music platform and give you 100% of your earnings. They also Give record deals to artists they really like.

Ditto. Ditto impresses me. They genuinely care about their artists, they have the best pricing for what they give you, and they offer a unique thing to the music distribution market: Playlisting. They push your music to Spotify and apple music playlist curators and they genuinely help get you discovered. And they get your music videos out too.

And last but not least: **Indiefy.** Indiefy is a free-25$ monthly Distribution service that has a super great customer service. They offer a lot for their free plan including distribution, and 85% of your royalties. Here's a helpful list of music distributers.

As soon as your music is out, you'll want to get two apps: Spotify for artists and Apple music for artists. These apps let you update how your music page looks, and they get you daily stats on your music.

Chapter 4: Fantastic beats and where to find them

Producers play a very important role in the music world. They delicately design the canvas for artists to paint on. The 2 places you can find beats are Beatstars.com and YouTube. Beware you cant just download a beat and release a song with it. You'll need a license for it, and that can range from a dollar to a thousand dollars. You'll be able to find a lot of great beats with good pricing on producers' websites. If you can't afford beats there are many quality beats for free. But beware, there's a difference between beats marked FREE and beats marked FREE FOR PROFIT. With a free beat you can get your song on platforms that won't pay you. Like SoundCloud or YouTube without add revenue. Free for profit means as long as the producer is given credit, you can release the song on all music platforms. I've been lucky to work with so many great producers. H3 music, Prophxcy and Derek

Minor to name a few.

Chapter 5: The Legal Stuff.

This is where the fun begins. (not really. this subject is super boring but really really really important) When you copyright a song, you're claiming ownership of said song. Whenever you finish writing, and recording a song its copyrighted under the sound recording (or the "master") copyright. You own that song and people can't copy it. After the "master" copyright there's also the **Music composition copyright.** The music composition copyright is ownership of the lyrics and beat, and its normally split 50/50 between the artist and producer.

Publishing Is revenue streams that come from these copyrights. There are five revenue streams that come from them:

Printing rights- the fee people owe you if they print your song for sheet music

Performance Royalties: royalties due to you anytime someone preforms or broadcasts your song in public

Sampling royalties- fee due to you whenever someone samples a part of your song for theirs

Mechanical royalties- royalties due to you whenever your music is put on a CD, Streamed, or purchased.

synchronization licenses- fee owed to you if your music is ever in a movie or on T.V.

Woah. Aye, that's a lot of revenue for one person to collect. Thankfully if you don't have the time or energy to collect all that revenue, you can enter a publishing deal. The publishing company will collect all of your royalties worldwide for a fee of about 30% of royalties.

That's a lot. I would encourage you to do what I've done and establish your own publishing company and register it with a performance rights organization.; like ASCAP, or BMI. They'll collect all of your performance royalties. Then set up an admin agreement with a reliable publisher. I literally only scratched the surface, and I highly suggest looking into publishing and copyrights further. Also check out this service: www.songtrust.com song trust collects ALL of your music royalties. They are used by people like Kato on the track, futuristic, and me.

Chapter 6: Marketing, Merch and shows: Get your name out there!

I'll separate this chapter into three parts

MAKETING

MERCH

SHOWS

Part one: MARKETING

So, your music is out and you're damn proud of it, but there's one problem. You literally only have like 3 plays on Spotify, and all of them are most likely from you. How the heck will you promote your music?!

Step one: get social media.

Regardless of how you feel about it, social media is an invaluable asset when promoting your music, growing a fanbase and connecting with other artists. You don't need an account on literally every platform though. The two

ESSENTIAL platforms are Facebook and Instagram. They both work hand in hand and you can connect your accounts. These are important platforms, because you can set up a *Musician/Band* account. This is important for two reasons: it helps anyone who comes across your page to identify you as an artist, and it establishes your page as a *Business*. With a business account, you can pay for targeted *add campaigns* through Facebook. Add campaigns send customized adds for your music to the targeted audiences feed. This can range from $1 to $1000 depending on how large and effective and wide-spread you want the campaign to be.

Step 2: promote your track.

There are three main ways to promote your track. Playlisting, Dorgod, (my personal favorite promotion company) and friends.

PLAYLISTING.

On Spotify, one of the main ways music fans discover new music is through Spotify playlists. There are playlists for all sorts of genres, moods and times. As soon as you distribute your tack, before it comes out, the Spotify for artists website will allow you to submit your song to Spotify editors for playlist consideration. You can only submit one song at a time so make sure its your best track. Mixed, and mastered are a must. Playlists will also determine which artists appear on the RELATED ARTISTS section of your page. So as far as the algorithm is concerned, you are who your playlisted next to.

DORGOD.

DorGodPromotions.com in no way sponsors this book. Just a disclaimer.

I've been more than privileged to work with Dorian and his team on some of my biggest projects. (beatsmas, hey there, and look at you tho! To name a few) when you submit your track to them, they'll promote it through their string of 1000+ DJs. Those DJs will actively play your song at all their venues. If you ordered a 10,000-play promotion and it's a good song, you'll easily get 12,000. If you ordered 10,000 plays and it's a GREAT song, you'll probably get 15,00 or more.

FRIENDS.

friends are the best way to promote music. No cap. Hands down. Best way. All you need are 4 or 5 friends who are willing to network your music, wear your merch, and stream your releases, and you will be very well off as far as brand new artist come. Speaking of merch, that brings us to

Part two: MERCH

Merchandise comes in many shapes and forms, and is made available by everyone from large companies and brands, to youtubers, musicians and more. Merchandising is also 1 of your three most important sources of income as a music artist. (Merch, shows and streaming revenue) what is merch? Its items such as hats, shirts, hoodies, coffee mugs, stickers, water bottles…etc. any essential the everyday consumer, you should consider a merchandising opportunity. Here's an example of a merch store:

https://teespring.com/stores/young-kaso.

Part 3: SHOWS

Playing shows isn't just a great way to get your name out there; it can also be your number one source of revenue as an artist. There are many show venues you can rent out for a show in most cities. If you can't afford to play at a venue, id suggest reaching out to slightly bigger artists about playing an opening act for them. You may have to pay to open for them, but I personally have never paid to play.

There are four things that you should expect about your first show to keep in mind:

1: YOU WILL BE NURVOUS

Its perfectly normal for you to be as scared as shit stepping up to the stage for the first time. Most artists are still nervous preforming for a crowd the 50th time. Use that adrenaline to go harder and always remember to have fun. If you have fun while preforming, the crowd will reflect the same energy.

2: THERE WON'T BE A LARGE CROWD

The harsh reality is that very few fans will turn up for your fist show. This is natural. Be sure to promote your performance everywhere you can. Posters, flyers, Instagram area targeted adds. These are great way to promote a show.

Keep the tickets cheap. Like 5$ cheap. Your first 50 shows will not be for money. They'll be getting your name out there. There's a large chance that the people who show up to your show, or a show your opening for, have never heard of you or your music. So, say your artist name repeatedly. I discovered some of my favorite music artists through show openings where they DOMINATED the stage, and when the main artist came out, everyone wanted to see the opening act again.

3: YOUR FIST SHOW WILL NOT BE GOOD.

Unless you've had a shit ton of experience stage acting or preforming in front of crowd for rap battles or family gatherings, your first show will probably suck. That's normal. The more you expect it to suck the less hard the feedback will hit. And if its good, you'll be pleasantly surprised. Always remember to bring a hype man on stage.

Someone who knows all the lyrics you'll be preforming. They'll finish the sentences if you run out of breath. My hype man is a old friend of mine. Always bring your instrumentals on a laptop hooked up to the sound system. Always have a close friend or relative running the sounds.

4: YOU WILL GET EXPOSURE

The main reason to do shows is to get your name out there. Always say your name or have people chant it. I've seen great opening acts that forgot to say their name and missed out on hundreds of potential fans. Don't be that guy.

All in all, your music is great, so it needs exposure. I listed what I've found to be the best ways to promote your music. There are plenty of other way that you can earn exposure but this is a very experience-based business. Live and learn!

Chapter 7: Getting to Know Your Fans

Your first fans will be your best friends. Then the more you promote and get your name out there, the more you'll notice random strangers showing you love. Welcome to the big wide world of having a fanbase. A strong Fanbase might me the number one most important thing to have in order to make it in the music industry.

Its extremely important to make every fan feel a personal connection to you. My number one rule is to treat every fan like family. That could be anything from giving backstage passes or show tickets to someone who cant afford it, to responding to comments and DMs. Take a hour a day for fan interaction.

Chapter 8: Budgeting and how to price stuff

Its really important to know how to price your albums,

merch. And show tickets.

You don't want to be too expensive, but you also want to

make money.

Here how I price an album with 10 songs: each song Is $1.99.

if a fan where to buy the song individually that would cost

well over $15. But for a ten-track album, with tracks of that

price, I charge $7. This makes the costumer get a sense of

saving money. Physical albums should be around $10.

Merchandise clothing such as hats, shirts and hoodies should

be a little over $20. Always make sure each music project

you come out with has its own budget for features, studio

time, and distrubition.

Chapter 9: Record Labels

This book is a guide to make it in the music industry

independently. However, if you feel that a record deal is right for your career, here's everything you need to know about record deals.

Record deals are the most important thing when it comes to most artists dream of making it in the music industry. The most important thing when signing to a label is to make sure you fare getting a fair deal. KNOW YOUR MUSICS WORTH! I've seen artists with the best music sign 20$ record deal where the label keeps 40% of the royalties. This is ridiculous. My advise based off of experience is to not sign a deal where the label takes more than 10%. Some labels will sign you with a RECOUPABLE deal. This means they will pay you a certain amount in advance and they will take your royalties until that amount is paid back. Avoid these deals unless it's a big label that will market your music well. Some labels offer 360 deals. A 360 deal is where the label will allow you to keep a good chunk of your music royalties, merch royalties, and show earnings. Remember don't sign your life away. You DON'T want to be in a one hit wonder situation. I've seen many of my friends sign a bad deal, make one charting song, then get put on hold by the label, never being able to release music again. my advice Is to stay independent. Keep all of your royalties. Its worth it in the long run, it just takes more time to blow up.

Chapter 10: Branding

Branding Is a huge part of being a musician. It helps people recognize you. You can build your branding by figuring out what you love. Do you love movies? Make your album art and photoshoots movie themed! Set up a catchphrase with a quote from your favorite movie! Catchphrases are pretty important to your branding. For instance, my catchphrase Is "Yo, its Kaso". Pretty simple but it helps people recognize me. Another thing I do for branding is, every one of my albums covers tell a story. Each cover has key colors, items, and references to songs that fit the concept for the album. While branding, you may have noticed that your musician name Is extremely important. It keeps you unique from everyone else in the industry. This is why its important to COPYRIGHT your name. the method to do that is to BECOME A BISUNESS. Go to legalzoom.com and set up your brand name as a company name. this helps you take legal action against anyone who tries to use your name.

Chapter 11: Advice

At the time I'm writing this I have been in the music industry
for 3 years as a manger, artist, agent, and publicist. So, I have
a crap ton of experience (even though I'm still leaning some.)
here's some of the best advice I ever got.

Before you release music, hone your skills. Make like 50
songs and learn your style THEN release your first song.

Don't give into fake promotions scams. There are many
scams (like Spotify jedi) that gibe convincing story's about
how effective their promo service is. Don't buy it. If you

think your getting bot plays on a song, stop the service. Any music platform will ban you.

Don't let your career consume you. Spend time with friends and family. Music is great but its not worth spending ALL of your time on. Trust me.

Take time to help smaller artists.

Practice your voice. Spend time exercising it. It's very important for your voice to be at its best when preforming, recording, and being asked to freestyle.

Come up with rhymes for everything you see. I drive myself crazy with it. It will improve your lyrical ability SO much. Treat EVERYBODY with respect.

Don't start beef.

Make industry connections. You are who you hang with.

You are only one song away from success. Don't give up.

That's just a few extremely important advice snippets! Keep them in mind.

That's all from me. Please reach out to me on Instagram (@Its_Kaso) if you need anything. I'm here to help you achieve your dream bro.

Acknowledgments

Thank you first and foremost to Raine Shich for being there for me when I needed you. Thank you to Raze, BlockBoiPoc, Hunter, Ezra, Daniel, Victorian, dark skies, and all of the pariah records family. Thanl you to Matthew Tuck, Skydxddy, Ashton Mallory, DM and futuristic. They say you never meet your heroes, but I'm proud to call mine friends. Thank you to mom and dad for teaching me anything is possible, and thank you to my whole Young Kaso team!

Thank you to Jeremiah and Jenna for being great friends.

And thank you to all of the reader for spending time reading

my ramblings about the music industry! It takes one song to

change a life! Even lil nas x only had 2,000 followers when

he dropped old town road. Your almost there- YK

About the author

Young Kaso (aka Matthew Rader) is a rapper and producer,

who's songs have gone viral on Spotify time and time again.

He currently resides in his home studio in castle rock,

Colorado.

www.ingramcontent.com/pod-product-compliance
Lightning Source LLC
Chambersburg PA
CBHW040928110726
48006CB00001B/111